Grace Is Everywhere

March 8, 1999

Dear Rita —
    Hope you enjoy these pages —
maybe some day you can
come here and see the place.
It's beautiful —
    all best wishes to you —
            James.

Grace Is Everywhere

Reflections of an Aspiring Monk

James Stephen Behrens, OCSO

James Stephen Behrens

ACTA

ASSISTING CHRISTIANS TO ACT

PUBLICATIONS

Grace Is Everywhere
Reflections of an Aspiring Monk
by James Stephen Behrens, OCSO

Edited by Patrice J. Tuohy
Cover design by Tom A. Wright
Cover photo by Karen Leibnitz
Typesetting by Garrison Publications

Copyright © 1999 by James Stephen Behrens, OCSO

Published by: ACTA Publications
Assisting Christians To Act
4848 N. Clark Street
Chicago, IL 60640-4711
773-271-1030

Library of Congress Catalog Number: 98-74566

ISBN: 9-87946-195-0

Printed in the United States of America

03 02 01 00 99 5 4 3 2 1 First Printing

Contents

Dedication

I want to dedicate this, my first book, to Mom and Dad, who by their faith called me to embrace the life that is born with each second, each turn of the wheel, each beat of the heart. Their love has long encouraged me to reach for what I can never hope to possess or understand: that wondrous mystery toward which we all move.

Foreword

When I was a young woman reading *Seven Storey Mountain* by Thomas Merton, the world of Trappist monasteries held both fascination and fear. Fascination won the day, however, because I somehow knew that the world of silence and long hours of prayer, the world of spare diets and mystical awareness was not to be my world. I could look at the mystery of Trappist life from afar, in perfect safety. It was something like reading the martyrology—I was thrilled that such bravery existed and grateful that I would not be called to exercise it.

But with the increase of years and responsibilities, my repertoire of Cistercian literature also increased. I began to discover in monastic life some clues for ordering my own decidedly lay life—one filled with growing children, changing relationships, community service, workplace duties, and a longing to know God in some experiential way. I read that in the beginning monasteries were referred to as "households of faith." Was that not exactly what my husband and I were hoping to create for ourselves, our children, and all those whose lives intertwined with ours?

I supplemented my reading with visits to a nearby Trappist monastery. There I found men who—like myself—had all kinds of daily tasks to

1

accomplish, a web of human relationships that required faithfulness to maintain, and the need to learn to recognize God in the progress of their ordinary days and nights.

A deepening knowledge of monastic spirituality helped my husband and me to name the priorities we had for our own particular household of faith. Solitude is one of those priorities. Because family life is intensely communal (as is monastic life), some attention to solitude is essential. Monks have their chapel or nearby woods—places to simply be with God. Laypeople, especially busy parents, may need to carve out such space. For both monk and layperson, solitude is not a luxury but a necessity in the quest for a balanced life. (Many Trappist monasteries, like the one in Conyers, have guest houses where men and women may come for a retreat and participate in the daily schedule of community prayer while they drink in the stillness and the solitude.)

Another priority my husband and I recognized as essential is stability—the virtue that grounds monks in the reality of everyday life. It does the same for families. Like the monastics, family members choose to cast their lots with imperfect others, to belong and to stick to one another in spite of all the idiosyncrasies and annoyances that abound in daily life.

When "worldly" Christians see how prayer (alone and with others), study, work, equality, authority and hospitality are adhered to in monastic settings, we can discern how we must order our own lives. One way that monks help us is through their own reflections and writings. *Grace Is Everywhere: Reflections of an Aspiring Monk* is a substantial contribution to understanding the mutuality between monastic life and ordinary households of faith. Father James Behrens, OCSO, has crafted these short essays as a kaleidoscope, allowing us to observe through them different facets of the sacred in the ordinary. His lens catches the stuff of life and holds it to the light of grace.

Household chores are an example. Many daily tasks are repetitive and monotonous, and most of us find ways to resist them. Behrens tells how he himself gained some insight into the value of boring work in "On Watering Plants" (p. 93). When assigned to water the monastery plants for four hours a day, he at first felt that he was just wasting time. That changed as he concentrated on the plants, discovering that each one required a different method of watering. He learned to distinguish between "good" bugs and "not so good" bugs. And he learned something else, something of lasting value—namely, that there are forms of work that must be done without hope of getting something back. "I now realize," he writes, "that such activity is how life itself thrives and blooms."

That particular vignette reminds me of a passage in Henri Nouwen's *Genesee Diary,* an account of the year he spent in a Trappist monastery in upstate New York. The abbot there assigned Nouwen to the job of loading rocks onto a pickup truck for several hours every afternoon. One day, Nouwen went to the abbot and said the rock loading was boring him beyond endurance. He wanted out. The abbot seemed pleased and replied that Nouwen's task was accomplishing its purpose and advised him to get "underneath" the boredom. I remember reading this passage at a time when I was folding dozens of diapers every day (this was in the pre-Pampers era.) I, too, was bored, but the abbot's words found resonance with me. I tried to become more attentive to my daily chore, and I found myself thinking about the countless men and women whose lives are measured by repetition. Suddenly, my isolation was pierced.

Like Nouwen, Behrens enables us to make connections in unlikely places. For example, Behrens' obvious love for the elderly monks at the Monastery of the Holy Spirit can help those of us who are trying to find ways to incorporate older parents, as well as elderly aunts and uncles and friends into our busy lives. Behrens shows us that practicing gentle respect seems the best way.

In his short piece "Edmund's Eyes" (p. 75), the author describes one evening at Compline, the final formal prayer time of the Trappists' day. The scene occurs in the darkened monastery church, with only an image of the Virgin Mary illumined. It is the old monk Edmund's turn to read a prayer. He finds his way to the lectern and stands there for several minutes turning the pages. Finally, he says softly and simply, "I cannot see." Then he repeats it more loudly. A younger monk, Joseph, comes to the lectern and reads the prayer, while the old monk stays silently by his side. In Behrens' telling of the tale, the younger monk becomes, for the moment, Edmund's eyes. "I am theoretically aware that we are one body here," he says. "I know the theology behind it and the long tradition of Christian sources that support the notion of oneness among many members. That night when Edmund said that he could not see, however, I experienced how he was literally given eyes by Joseph and how the rest of us were given a sense of what we can and do mean to one another."

Such simple gestures are the heart of a community—whether monastic or familial. And who of us, at whatever age, would not be grateful for them?

Grace Is Everywhere, amazing in its simplicity and transparency, is filled with like examples that can help all of us to see and hear the quiet movements of the Holy Spirit in the most commonplace of experiences.

In that it hints at poetry.

Dolores Leckey
Woodstock Theological Center
Georgetown University
Washington, D.C.

Introduction

My parents named me Jeff, which is how most people back in New Jersey know me. When I was very young, my mom took my sisters and brothers and me to New Orleans to visit relatives. We traveled by train. Dad stayed home because he had to work and could not get time off. The train was called the Southerner. I remember parts of that long train ride: the scenes that glided past the large train window, the warm and friendly face of a porter, the tall soft cushioned seats. I can still see the end cars winding far behind as I looked at them from the window whenever the train took a wide, slow curve.

During our stay in New Orleans, Mom took us to Audubon Park, which was not far from where she grew up and where her parents then lived. There was a large carousel there. I remember standing before that wonderful-looking ride. I looked with awe at everything about it: the painted wooden animals—horses and lions, zebras and bears—and the large seats that were carved into the shapes of ornate sleds, all fastened to shiny poles. They moved up and down on the poles as the carousel turned, and organ music played from a real pipe organ at its center. Row after row of colored light bulbs were strung across the roof, flashing red, blue, yellow and green with the rising and falling of the wooden animals.

Someone—perhaps Mom or an attendant at the carousel—helped me onto a large wooden horse. The horse was painted a shiny brown and there was a leather strap that was fastened around my waist. The ride began, the music started, and to my delight as so many things moved about me I, too, moved up and down on the horse, holding on to the shiny pole. The park about me slowly glided past trees and paths and the small crowd standing at the gates of the carousel. They were waiting for the next ride in the heat of that long-ago summer's day. I felt like the center of a moving and beautiful world, a world of lights and music and handsomely carved animals. What a ride it was, and perhaps is now, if that carousel is still there. I have been back to New Orleans many times since, but it has been a long time since I went to Audubon Park.

I still like rides of all sorts. As the years have passed, I have gradually discovered that there are many things to learn from rides. Physicists tell us that the universe is moving, that the cosmos itself is in motion, so—in the most grandiose terms possible—all that we know and love is riding along, coming from someplace and going somewhere. Little did I know as I rode that carousel that the stars far above me were moving as surely as were those colored lights right above my head.

It was easy to hold the reins of that wooden

horse, and rise and fall and turn. It was also easy to sit and look out the window of the Southerner as it made its way through cottonfields and bayou country. But as I have grown over the years, the ride that is life has not always been as easy.

Much of my life has been a struggle to find and keep a certain balance. I suppose that the same could be said of any human life. We all want a smooth ride, a ride shared by those we love and who love us, a ride soothed by music and graced with color all around. We want to know where we are coming from and where we are going.

I am a Trappist monk and have lived in the cloistered monastery in Conyers, Georgia for just over four years. When I entered the novitiate, I took the name James in honor of my brother. I came here by train and remember noting that the founding monks who built this monastery also traveled here by train from Gethsemani, Kentucky, just over fifty years ago. Before I moved here, I was a priest of the Archdiocese of Newark for twenty years. I wrote the following vignettes while here in Conyers.

One morning, after completing the manuscript, I went for a ride. It was a ride with Damian, one of the monks, and it suddenly occurred to me that riding has been a key part of my life. Rides from heres to theres—on carousels and cars and planes and trains and boats—rides with bumps and lights and family and friends and ups and downs. There have been inner rides as well, rides of the heart, movements of hope and love, paths of joys and sorrows, journeys of regrets and gratitudes. I have wandered along ways of selfishness and ignorance and taken some dead ends that really hurt. But they have all been part of the ultimate mystery ride that is life.

I want to share with you the place where my ride has brought me—the Monastery of the Holy Spirit. If you ever come here, we can ride a bit, and I will show you what there is to see and experience, but you would have to stay a while and let your mind and heart journey a bit on your own.

Chances are you will not be able to do that. So, I offer the following words as my only way of taking you along with me and sharing with you some of the daily experiences of life here. There are no colored lights or shiny wooden horses at the monastery, though we do have some nice music and beautiful stars. And we monks, too, have our ups and downs. But it is a good ride, all things considered—kind of like a monastic carousel, spinning toward God, on which all that is truly human can be found and loved.

The following reflections are movements from one place to another, movements from one person's heart to the hearts of others, and, taken all together, the movement from this life to life eternal. It is for me a recurring and stunning realization that the journey of life is eternal, a ride through all that is human to that which is divine.

People who stay for a time in our retreat house often comment as to how still the monastery is. I well remember experiencing that when I came here and inquired about the life more than twenty years ago. I took a ride here and liked what I saw. But it was not time yet for me to seriously consider entering the cloister, so I rode back to New Jersey and served in several parish assignments. Then the time was right, or seemed to be, and here I am. Having lived here for a while now, I can better understand the treasure that is here. Those who visit often find that our way of life appeals to them because it allows them to slow down and find a deeper or different kind of meaning in their busy days. I often see a man or woman sitting in a chair down beside our lake, just gazing at the movement of the water and taking in the peace that this place affords. I find, though, that I want to tell visitors that the life here has its own bumps. In a culture that so prizes activity and motion to gauge accomplishment, living a simple day-to-day routine that is devoid of the typical marks of success takes some getting used to. We monks pray, study, work . . . and stay put. But, as I have found, such a simple routine can enhance and bring to the surface of one's heart those things that are the essence of life. Faith, hope and charity are what human beings really hunger for. Nothing else really matters. The monastic life is nothing but an expression of and an attempt to live what really matters.

Damian's Stone

Surrey Lane was the dead-end street on which I spent the early years of my life. It is the first place I remember as a "place."

We used to get bread delivered by a driver we called the Duggan Man, because Duggan's was the brand name of the bread. He was a happy and friendly man. He would stop in front of our house and go into the back of his truck and load up his tray with bread for several houses. He let us kids climb onto the truck and peek into its spacious rear.

Along the inner walls of the Duggan Man's truck were shelves, stacked neatly with rows of bread, cakes, cupcakes, coffee rings, doughnuts and cookies. The smell was wonderful. All of the boxes had cellophane tops, so it was easy to see what was in them. The iced tops of the cupcakes—soft, luscious-looking mounds and swirls of chocolate, vanilla and strawberry—always looked better than the ones our mothers made.

(I am sure that we kept that opinion to ourselves, however.) My family usually got just a few loaves of bread, except for special occasions when the Duggan Man would take a cake off the shelf and deliver it to our house.

Every now and then, the Duggan Man would give us a ride. It wasn't a long ride, just a block or so to his next stop, and we stood right next to him and stared out the window at the concrete lane passing beneath the wheels. With a friendly "See you next time," the Duggan Man would help us off the truck and be on his way. It was always good to see him.

And there was the Milk Man, whose name we never knew either. He delivered for Borden's milk, and his truck was just like the Duggan's bread truck, except that it was a shiny silver color and a bit more beat up. The Milk Man came very early in the morning. On Saturdays, not school days, we would run out and greet him as he came up the street. I remember the inside of that truck, too, with its rows of glass-bottled milk, kept cool by big chunks of ice that were so clear we could see right through them. The Milk Man delivered milk and cream and juices. He would fill each order from a paper that his customers filled out and left in one of the empty bottles that he picked up the day before. He carried the fresh bottles in a metal basket, with little compartments of just the right size for the different types of bottles.

The empties were left in metal milk boxes that each family kept outside, usually near the kitchen door. He would take the empties and replace them with the fresh bottles, each with a picture of Elsie the Cow, Borden's logo, stamped in red on the glass. I wonder what happened to all those milk boxes.

Mom usually placed an order just for milk, except maybe once a week when she would get a small pint bottle of heavy cream to make whipped cream. If one (or more) of us was sick or if there was a birthday, she would place an order for a quart or two of chocolate milk.

The Milk Man gave us rides, too, and I loved the sound of the jingling of the bottles as they shifted back and forth in their metal crates. The inside of the truck was cold and even in the summer months the Milk Man wore a jacket. He always stood while driving, as did the Duggan Man. All the kids on Surrey Lane wanted to grow up to be like the Milk Man and the Duggan Man. I think that we sensed that there was something good in what they did. They brought good things to people, and they seemed to have a great time doing it.

Even though I could never have expressed it in words back then, I think that what I was learning was that to get anywhere you might need help, and the best help is freely given.

Much of this came back to me one day while sitting in the woods here at the monastery. The memories did not come all at once, but there was a singular event that was like a key that opened a door in my heart to memories that had always been there but had been long asleep.

The event was nothing extraordinary. It was the starting of the engine of a van. It belongs to Damian, one of our monks. He parks the van behind the retreat house, up the hill just a little ways from where I usually sit in the mornings. I did not think much about it the first time I heard the sputter, cough, wheeze and then engagement of the engine as it came to life with Damian's expertise. But the noise came to signal for me the start of another day, even more so than the monastery bell that rings at ten each workday morning. When Damian's van comes to life, it does so with a reel and a rock, and it brings me to life, too.

The van is filled with all sorts of fascinating things: empty aerosol cans, screwdrivers, oily rags, old jackets, a Mexican sombrero, a long red plastic horn, chains, hammers and tools of all shapes, ages and purposes. There are rolls of tape and old newspapers, boxes and boxes of a hundred sizes of nails and screws; metal pipes, pieces of glass, gas and electrical meters with the wires hanging loose. It contains scraps of metal, old shoes, an old battered lunch box and thermos, old blankets—indeed everything one might need to get through a day.

There is a magical quality to Damian's van. Its disarray has a beauty, a purpose that I intuit more than understand. I know that there is no other truck like his. And I also know that Damian is as unique as his van.

One morning I was walking on a road down by a hay field and I heard the van coming up behind me. I turned around and watched as it neared me. It swayed a bit as Damian maneuvered over the bumpy road. Damian's two dogs, Sasso and Bozo, occupied places of honor in front of the van. Sasso's head was sticking out the open window of the side door and Bozo was standing on his hind legs looking out the front window at the oncoming world, his paws planted firmly on the dashboard amid the empty aerosol cans. Bozo and Sasso are mutts. They are good dogs and have a good life here. Damian takes good care of them, and they know it.

Damian pulled up next to me and asked me to hop in. I climbed into the van and after being generously licked and pawed by Bozo and Sasso, I found a place to lean and off we went. We did not go very far—just up toward the Abbey store, along the road that winds down toward the barns, and then down to the rear of the property back to the large garage where Damian has his shop and the dogs have their pen.

Damian and I chatted a bit about the weather and some other daily interests. He then asked me whether I liked the monastic life. I looked at him, smiled and said yes I did. And it was at exactly that moment that memories of other rides I have taken began to focus more clearly. I gradually remembered with vividness the Milk Man and the Duggan Man. It was not an immediate flash of recognition, but more like a very warm and familiar sense that I had been on rides like this before, and there seemed to be a continuity, a good continuity that I wanted to understand.

So I sat in the woods on many mornings after that ride, and when I heard the sputter and roar of Damian's van, I thought about the rides that we kids had on Surrey Lane, and many other rides that I have taken. It occurred to me that we monks travel along a common track. In that alone, we mean much to each other. The Latin *monos* may mean "alone," but we are alone in a very close togetherness. We journey together in solitude.

I now carry in my pocket a smooth oval stone that Damian gave to me. He saw me admiring it in his van and asked if I wanted one. I said yes, that it was beautiful. The next day there were four of them in my mail drawer. "Give two to your sisters and one to your mom," he said. He laughed, and then told me that they were worry stones.

It is typical of Damian to give four when asked for one. When I feel the stone in my pocket, I think of him, and of goodness and happiness, and of my sisters and our mom. It is for me not a worry stone but a memory stone.

I use Damian's stone as a stepping stone to God—as a reminder that God remembers me, even though I often forget God. I finger the stone and find it holds many warm memories. And then I say a prayer to God, who remembers always and forever.

There is a gospel account of Jesus telling the disciples about the goodness of God. If a son asks his father for bread, Jesus says, the father will not give him a stone. If a man is that good, the story implies, then how much greater is the goodness of God.

Perhaps I have been blessed with a good variation on that tale. I asked for a stone and was given just that. But the days of bread and milk and carefree rides now live in that stone in my pocket.

Missy's Ride

The place was called Bond's, and it was famous for miles around for its ice cream, hamburgers and big thick malts called Awful Awfuls. It was on Valley Road in Montclair, New Jersey, where a bank now stands. That is the town where I grew up. Bond's was once listed in *Esquire*, I think, as one of the top-ten hangout spots for teens in the country. I will never fathom why it was torn down. Business was always good. I thought that the place would last forever.

In the early Sixties, I must have spent the sum total of a year leaning against a bumper in the parking lot of Bond's or driving around the building, which was possible since there was only one-way traffic allowed in the parking lot. Once they exited the parking lot, most kids made an immediate right turn back onto Valley Road and drove right back into the parking lot. It was called "cruising around."

I can still hear Dad as I asked him for the

family car keys on Friday and Saturday nights.

"Well, Jeff," he would say, "Where are you going tonight?"

"Just driving around," I would reply.

"Driving around? What do you mean, driving around?"

I laundered my reply a bit. I would tell him that friends and I were just going to Bond's. But we did literally drive around many a night: around the parking lot, around the block, back to the parking lot. Around and around, again and again—like that Chuck Berry song, "Round 'n' Round."

There were summer nights when well over a hundred kids hung out in that parking lot. The smell of English Leather and Canoe, popular colognes in those days, hung heavily in the air. The cars were polished and flashy. Chinos were "in" for both genders, and the Beach Boy look was very much in vogue: Madras shirts, no shoes, full heads of hair. The Beatles and Stones were just starting to make it big, and it would not be long before our own hair grew longer and the music shifted from bebop to Liverpool. Bob Dylan's "Like a Rolling Stone" blared from the juke box, which also carried a hefty number of selections from Dion and the Belmonts, the Four Seasons, and other "safe" groups that would soon struggle to find a place on the music charts as rock music was being revolutionized.

My brother, Jimmy, and I took turns driving our white Chevrolet Impala—its soft green dash board lights casting an iridescent glow and the windshield reflecting the streetlights outside. Our friends Greg and Walter sat in the back. I cannot help but think that our chats were pretty sophisticated for high-school kids. Or maybe our dads were right: maybe we just *thought* we were smart. I wonder, as we go through life do we always think we possess some sort of cutting-edge insight into the way things really are?

Once we arrived at Bond's, we would stay for hours just hanging out and doing nothing. We had no big worries. There was a lot of music blaring from the cars. Pretty girls that we boys dreamed about were everywhere. Those July and August nights seemed like the longest and most carefree times I have ever known. Life could not have been kinder. Joe Walsh, of the musical group the Eagles, used to hang out at Bond's. I even played several times with him in a high-school band called the Nomads, which is my only claim to near fame.

That was more than thirty years ago, as were those long, carefree rides on summer nights. Or so I thought.

A few days ago, a little girl named Missy came with her grandmother Anne to help wrap bonsai pots for us here at the monastery, which is one of our industries here, along with a bakery, a stained-glass shop and a religious goods and bookstore.

Missy took a liking to a golf cart that we use to move pots from one location to another and begged and begged for a ride. I could not turn her down, so she hopped in next to me and we took a ride around the monastery property. She gushingly told me that she was nine and that she could not wait to drive, to be a grownup. She showed me her multicolored fingernails. On each nail was a different design. She stretched her fingers and wiggled them. I smiled at the rapid movement of the tiny stars, rainbows, daisies and teardrops. I told her that I really understood what she meant about not wanting to wait to grow up, because there was a place called Bond's that I used to go to when I was just a bit older than she was. She asked me what I did there. I told her not much—just looked at pretty girls and tried to act cool.

She nodded her head and giggled knowingly. She asked me whether Bond's was around here. I told her no, not really, but that those kind of places find you when you need them. They are like rides in a golf cart. She looked at me, and then at her nails, thought for a moment, and said, "Uh-huh." Which I think meant yes.

Later that night I went for a long walk with Brother Mark, one of our monks. I thought of Missy, of growing up, of rides and walks and carts and bumpers, and of how many reincarnations of Bond's have come my way.

Hannah at the Train Station

On my way to enter the monastery, I hitched a ride from New Jersey and stayed with my sister Meg and her family in Herndon, Virginia. She and my brother-in-law Jim have three children: Emily, Hannah and Chris. Hannah is the youngest. She was then about five years old.

I stayed in my nephew's room. Chris, then nine, amazed me with his tidiness. Everything was in order. On the ceiling in his bedroom were dozens of phosphorescent stars of different shapes that glowed in the night. The ceiling was like a planetarium. I lay awake and gazed at the cosmos above me, eventually lulled to sleep by radiant images.

Hannah sat with me in the mornings as we had breakfast. Her questions were many and amusing. She asked them in a singsong way. What is a monk? What is a monastery? Is it far?

Can we visit? Do they have kids? Is there a school? Are there animals? What is a Trappist? Does that mean they are trapped?

I thought about that last one for a while.

Hannah is a very friendly and intense little girl, and I sensed that many things were churning in her mind and would eventually emerge. Her little legs swung back and forth a mile a minute as she asked one question after another. She digested what I told her along with her Wheaties and seemed satisfied as she left for school.

On the morning that I departed for Conyers, I took Meg and Jim and the kids to lunch at Union Square Station, not far from the White House in D.C. It was beautifully renovated several years ago, and there are many nice restaurants and shops. It is fun to sit and watch all the people coming and going. The ceilings are high and all the sounds of a train terminal echo throughout, adding a nice backdrop to the smaller intimate conversations taking place at the bars and tables.

Hannah fussed over her menu and eventually trusted Meg's choice for her: a hamburger and a Coke.

I knew that it would be a long time before I would be back in Herndon again. A sense of a change in our lives and ties as a family was in the air. My departing by train for Georgia was bringing all of us no small amount of heartache. It was painful because we did not know when we would next see one another.

I cannot remember what we talked about at lunch. Most surely it was small talk, carefully crafted to keep at a distance the sadness that was as real as the food before us.

Hannah pulled from her little purse a gift. It was a drawing of a lamb, done in crayons, with blue eyes and fuzzy brown fur (and, I think, shoes). She passed it to me proudly across the table and smiled. It was Lent, and I had seen the Lenten artwork from their religious-education classes taped to the refrigerator door in their kitchen. I think that she knew or remembered something about Jesus being called the Lamb of God and that impressed her. I still have the little work of art here in my room.

It was soon time to gather my belongings and catch the train. I walked to the van parked out in front, and when it came time to say goodbye to Hannah, she threw her arms around my neck and kissed me and started to cry. I was so surprised that so much had been welling up inside her. I hugged her and kissed her, and told her that I would see her soon and write to her and call her, and that Atlanta was not really very far. She sniffled and, after looking at Meg for a look of acceptance of the veracity of my words, smiled a bit and nodded her head. Her tears released the same sadness and pain in me, and I was a good while on the train before my insides settled.

The sadness of that separation has receded somewhat. Hannah was here to visit just a week ago and does not remember the paper lamb. She had a good time, though, and I will write her during the week.

I will thank her for loving me, and for being my niece, and for coming so far to see me. I will thank her for that day in the train station and will ask her whether she remembers all the people coming and going and sitting and eating and laughing and crying. And I will thank her again for hugging me and kissing me and crying.

And I will write her about the Lamb.

I will tell her that the Lamb is Jesus, and he gave his life for us, and is a part of us, and that we are a part of each other, and that is why we laugh and cry. It hurts to be apart and feels good to be together. I will ask her never to be afraid to feel love for everything and everyone, even if it hurts sometimes, and urge her to remember that even if who or what she loves changes or goes away it is important to still love. For not many things stay the same forever, except love.

Hannah may wonder about the why and the terrible beauty of such things. And then she will know why poets write, and songs are sung, and children are fascinated by lambs, and why I boarded a train to Georgia, with her paper lamb in my pocket and my neck still moist from her tears.

Carried by the Winds

On Sunday mornings, I usually gather a book or two and walk down to an old barn. There are several such barns here at the monastery, from the days when the monks had a dairy industry. The barns are now used for storage. One barn I particularly like is very spacious, and the rear of it opens to a large wooded area. There is a paved section in the back where I keep a lawn chair. Right next to the chair is a cinder block on which I can place my books and papers. A large iron gate is permanently open and rests against the wall. Ivy grows freely up the sides of the barn. Tree limbs have found their way into long broken windows. The wood is old and beautiful. Everything looks just right to me—a natural kind of decay and growth. It is peaceful there.

One Sunday, I had gathered my books and was making my way down to the barn when I noticed that the skies were darkening. It looked very threatening, as if the heavens were about to open. I was anxious to get to my favorite spot, though, so I decided to risk getting wet and started on my way. I was about halfway there when, with a crack of thunder, it started to pour. A strong wind blew in from seemingly nowhere, and I knew that a severe storm was imminent. I thought it best to seek shelter, and the nearest place was the small porch behind the monastery store. As small a place of refuge as it is, it would offer some shelter from the wind and the rain. I ran for it and had no sooner stepped under the roof when the rain came down in torrents, and the wind reached gale force. Trees were swaying and entire branches started to tear away from their bases and fly through the air every which way. I could do nothing but sit and wait it out and try to keep as dry as possible. I did not mind. It was something, that storm—how quickly it had arrived and how fierce it was. I liked watching it.

I marveled at how the wind forced so many things in its path to bend, to make way for its power. I saw what I thought were bits of paper or perhaps large leaves in the distance buffeted by the wind. But as they came closer, I realized that they were birds. I watched them, fascinated by how they seemed to have mastered a way to allow the wind to carry them. Even though they were tossed around a bit, they managed to aright themselves and move ahead, carried along by something far stronger than themselves. They had learned to make good use of the winds that carried them. I had the sense that even if the wind tired of them, it could not blow them from the sky. The birds knew too well how to maneuver, how to rise and fall and sway with every shift in the wind's direction and velocity. The birds passed above me, and then rode the winds on toward the main building.

Eventually the skies cleared, and I headed down to my chair in the barn, avoiding the large puddles and small rivulets of water that had formed so rapidly. By the time I got to my chair and sat down, little birds were bathing and drinking in the puddles behind the barn.

There are other winds that sometimes blow within me: winds of anxiety and worry, fear and mistrust, anger and regret. They can easily dislodge and disperse whatever peace I may think is mine.

Birds are wise. They do not flee the wind—they use it well, ride with it, and get where they need to go. They carry no books or papers or maps to guide them—just instinct that frees them to trust the wind.

A monastery is a place to become familiar with the winds, to grow wise as to their sudden appearance, ferocity and shifts in directions. The wisdom is to be still and not run, to befriend the winds and be carried by them. Eventually they bring us to places of refreshment and cleansing.

The Monk Who
Needs His Sleep

One day while I was chatting with Francis Michael, one of our monks, he told me how upset he was because he found it very difficult waking up for the early hour of vigils. The monastery bell rings at 3:45 every morning, and he occasionally sleeps through both that and his alarm. He revealed this to me one afternoon, after I had shared with him some things about which I had been very anxious.

I had wanted to speak with Francis because he is blessed with a receptive heart and a generous ear. When he walks into a room, a warmth enters with him.

When I first came to the monastery, the idea that Jesus prayed in me through his Spirit helped a lot. I wanted then and want now to let him "be" in me, and to use my life, my time, my words, my very self as he may see fit for his self-expression. Yet I still sense within me a strong attachment to finding the "right" words, the "right" time, the "right" everything. So I do not feel as trusting of Jesus as I perhaps should be. I know he is within me, even before I think of him or worry about his presence. So why do I not simply trust his movement in my heart?

It is easy for me to awake every morning. I do so much earlier than I need to. It comes naturally. I would like to think that as Jesus may need to awaken in me, he may need to sleep a while longer in the heart of my fellow monk. That Jesus lives in this monk is obvious.

Maybe I would be less anxious if I slept a bit more and worried less.

Singing with Tom

Brother Tom has a voice of pure gold. He is our cantor. The quality of his voice is as rare as it is good. He sings with his heart. Each word that he sings seems crafted and lingers in the air for a brief but beautiful moment and then fades gracefully to make room for the next word. When strung all together, the chant is divine expression. Tom's gift endows our chanting in choir with everything a seeker of prayerful psalmody could hope for. He brings to his words genuine expressions of joy, pain, loss and hope. They come from a place in his heart where he has known them. He takes the range of human experience that can be found in the psalms and lifts them from the text with the careful and tender use of his voice. His words carry these psalms from us to God.

I used to sit across from Tom in choir and loved to watch him sing. His eyes close as he sings. His right hand makes the slightest movements in the air, as if placing the perfectly pure notes in some magical place before him, where

they rest ever so briefly before taking flight after
the other still resonating notes.

I do not know whether Tom ever struggled
to find that voice that seems to come to him so
naturally. He does more than sing well. He knows
how to give certain words and phrases a haunt-
ingly exquisite cadence that is just slightly out of
syncopation with the organ, and the result is
something mystical.

Now, for the past few months I have been
sitting next to Tom in the choir, and he has been
gradually working me into the repertoire of
psalmody. I found one day that I was leaning
toward him, as if his voice was drawing me to
him, and a memory from long ago came back to
me that was painful in its vividness.

I used to sing with my twin brother, Jimmy,
who was killed in a car accident thirty years ago
(on his way home from Bond's ice-cream parlor
one night). We sang well together. Harmony
came easily to me. I would sing the high parts,
and Jimmy sang the low. Our voices were as iden-
tical as our faces, and I would always lean as close
to him as possible to keep on key. Jimmy's voice
was strong, and just singing with him enhanced
the strength, force and direction of my own.
Without my ever being aware of it, Jimmy was
crafting my voice, guiding and toning it. He was
making it like his own while at the same time
building my confidence.

I had long forgotten what it was like to sing with him, though I have so missed the life that we had together.

When that flashback happened and I realized who it was I last leaned into while I sang, my eyes filled with tears. I do not think that anyone saw. I pulled out a handkerchief and wiped my eyes and blew my nose as if I had a slight and sudden cold. But in a strange way, my heart was elated. I had once again found someone to truly sing with, and it is still a beautiful experience.

Not too long ago, Tom shared with me that he wanted to write and that he was struggling with words and ideas and sentences and, above all, confidence. I had heard him tell me stories about his youth, stories that were human and interesting, and I told him to trust his words and his memories and just write, and then write some more, and then go back and write again, and then pass it around to some people he trusts to get feedback. He is, in short, struggling to find a voice that does not come as readily to him as his chant voice.

I hope Tom can lean into me and write. The words are all around him, right next to that magical place in the air where he so lovingly places his notes.

Strange the things we carry about us, things that are very real and about whose presence and power we have little, if any, inkling. By loving song and being so generous with it, Tom actually improves the voices of others. He sings and others follow—and others sing more beautifully. It is that simple.

We teach one another every day, simply by doing what we love and in so doing impart our best.

The Living Cross

During a recent trip, our Abbot, Dom Bernard, lost his pectoral cross. He spoke about it during our Sunday morning chapter when he returned and said that he felt bad because of the many memories he associated with the cross. He explained the circumstances of its loss, and then said with gratitude and more than a trace of fondness that he hoped whoever finds it might benefit from it as much as he had.

I wondered as the abbot spoke if the cross would ever be found and returned. But as Dom Bernard let his possession go with a wish of well-being for its finder, something else stirred within me—a blend of admiration and guilt.

The more I get to know of my fellow monks, the more I admire the grace with which they give of everything, even their losses. Whoever finds Dom Bernard's cross will also find the special blessing that comes with everything he touches.

The more I get to know myself, on the other hand, the more I realize how far I have to go in learning to cope with even the little things I lose or have lost along the way. I am not sure how I will ever cope with the loss of bigger things—time, memory, my loved ones, my life itself.

I know that taking Jesus to heart is the secret to it all. I have learned as much from observing our monks. Knowing Jesus makes all kinds of losses bearable, even though such losses may cut very deeply into the heart.

The cross is a reminder that, try as we might to keep what we are and have, eventually we stand to lose it all. It is a freeing wisdom to live in such a way that our lives are transparent enough to allow God to shine through as the single truly important possession.

Every now and then we are graced with people who not only wear a cross but have learned to take it to heart. For most of my life, the best gifts I have received have been abstract things—realities that are self-contained. Peace, goodness, charity and hope, for example, have come my way only as I have experienced them in and through the lives of others.

Listening to Dom Bernard that morning, I suddenly realized that all gifts that are of God and given through the Spirit are the very life and reality of Jesus. He is peace, he is goodness, he is hope, he is charity. These do not exist apart from him.

"God alone." Those two words are a prayer that says it all.

The cross is a living, loving and redemptive mystery. The cross is the life of Jesus in each of us. If I learn to take my crosses to heart, I am allowing Jesus his rightful home there . . . and I can never lose him.

Peewee's Laugh

Peewee is a layman. He and I work together in the monastery, in the old barn where we store our bonsai pots. We wrap and ship bonsai pots and other accessories to places near and far. There was a major fire in that area last November, and since then we monks have needed all the help we can get. It might be said that the wind that fanned the fire that night in November kept on blowing long after the flames were put out, but in this case the bad winds turned good. They brought Peewee.

In an article about the late Frank Sinatra, the singer was quoted as saying that he often heard music and notes in his head and was mystified as to where such beauty came from. At times I experience such music, too, but there are times these days when laughter enters my mind as well. Peewee's laugh rings in my ears and lingers warmly within me long after he has gone home, and the thought of him laughing always makes me smile.

Peewee does not have much money and has not traveled much. I do not know whether he envies those who have. He has never said. He takes a delight in the simple, everyday things of life. I like to hear him speak of such things.

His laugh makes me wonder about what it means to be human.

We suffer from a strange vision of the ideal human as being complete, self-contained, fulfilled and satisfied. Then we strive to reach that goal ourselves. This road to the attainment of self-sufficiency is, for many of us, believed to be found through wealth. Yet the goal seems to be always just ahead of us, as if on a constantly receding horizon that never comes closer or gives way to our weary feet. No matter what we accumulate or from whom we ask directions, we never find happiness.

Peewee will never walk such a road. He is well on the way to somewhere else, laughing here and there along the way.

I suppose Peewee thinks me to be a religious man and considers this monastery to be a religious place. Yes, I think about God. And, yes, this place is special to anyone who comes here. I suppose that my being a part of it involves me in something religious. Yet the monastery is often a heady enterprise, a road of words and rituals and meetings and elevated discourse. But something in the very depths of our humanity bids us monks stop and look down at our very feet, at the road we are all on. Peewee's laughter, his lightheartedness and joy, invite us to listen to something of God that is different from the world's idea of human success.

The road to the Kingdom is toll-free. There is no "getting" it or even losing it. It is ours as we live it. We find it when we live from our incompleteness and our need for each other. It is an easy road to find. One of the signs that point the way is Peewee's laughter.

Abiding Beauty

The world will be saved by beauty.
–Peguy

One afternoon, I stood in what was once a beautiful garden. I had been told that it had been the pride and joy of a man who was now an old monk. I had seen photographs of it and indeed it was truly beautiful. Every imaginable color burst forth from so many plants and flowers. Paths cut through the garden, paths now overgrown with weeds and fallen leaves, but even the paths were laid out by the monk with an obvious eye for loveliness. They twisted and turned, carefully laid out beneath the shade of the large trees, no part of them exposed to the heat of the sun. There were several old benches on which no one rested anymore.

There are far fewer monks now than when the monk was young, and the ones that remain have little time to rest. When they do rest, it is done in other places on our grounds.

The monk's garden has long since been abandoned. I was there to tidy it up as best I could, but I did not know where to begin. I raked a bit, pulled a few weeds, and then sat on one of the benches. I heard a noise and turning around saw the old monk standing behind me, leaning on his cane and pointing out a particular tree to me. He smiled as he spoke and said that he had planted that tree years ago. His kind, blue eyes sparkled, and he seemed oblivious to the ruins that surrounded him. He whispered the name of the tree, a name I had never heard, with a kind of love. He raised his voice just a bit and continued to speak to me, telling me what plants were once where, and how he loved keeping the place beautiful. But, he said, he was now too old and had to let the garden go.

His hand must have grown tired, for he soon placed it on top of his other hand and leaned on his cane. The cane shook slightly. He smiled at me, told me to do what I could and then shuffled off.

Our years pass quickly. We are given just so much time and strength to tend our garden. With care and patience, beauty is trimmed and managed and brought to an artistically inspired fruition. The garden then stands proud and affords passers-by a place to sit and wonder about their lives. Then, like those lives, the garden fades.

Days later, near sunset, I entered the garden again and the old monk was sitting on a bench. He saw me and smiled, and, raising his cane, pointed to the setting sun, a huge ball of red fire sinking beneath a cloudy sky. "It is so beautiful," he said, and smiled again. I sat next to him, and we spoke for a while of the things of that day. He listened, but his eyes were fixed on the sun.

I have a feeling that my brother monk is now beyond all that surrounds him. There was once a sure reciprocity that existed between his concerns and his garden. He did his bit when it was time to do so, and now seemed to relish basking in a more enduring beauty, symbolized, perhaps, by the setting sun that would surely rise again the next morning.

Beautiful things indeed abound. Thank God for the many who create things of beauty and who open our eyes and hearts to all the beauty that there is. But there is another kind of beauty that is coming, that our years and cries summon, a beauty that shall seize us and enrapture us. It makes eyes sparkle and moves an old monk to whisper with love to a tree that will one day die.

Pablo's Song

Those who seek the solitude of the desert, who intentionally go off to a faraway place, do so because they feel drawn by the mystery of God. God whispers to them, and they leave all that is familiar. They retreat to listen and know better the One who calls, who whispers, who bids come

The monastery is not as remote or as desolate as a desert. There are, ironically, times when it is not even easy to find a genuine place of solitude. There are always sounds—of cars in the distance, of jets passing overhead, of church bells that toll. The raising of one's head can always afford a glimpse of a monk or two in the distance, quietly walking on one of the many paths here that wind through the woods. It is necessary, then, for a monk to find for himself a place set apart, a place that is his own, where the raising of his head affords nothing but a view of the trees and where the sound of cars and jets can seem distant enough to be a part of another world.

I have found such a place, deep in the woods, an easy walk from the main monastery buildings. I go there often and sit and let peace take hold of my heart and whisper what it will. The peace is not a voice but indeed a whole new language—a language that uses the wind as a tongue, the leaves as syllables, the birds as laughter, the bees as a hum, the greens and browns of the forest as tones of passion and desire, the smells and musty vapors of the dense woods as sweet breath.

Late one evening, I was sitting and listening in the woods to the birds and other creatures speak their languages. The day was done, and I do not know why the creatures speak then, for I know that they, too, rest at night, putting aside until the coming of the morning their search for mates and food. But the late evening is always a time for singing, too. I like to think that perhaps there are some lonesome doves among the animals who are hoping to find some comfort before the sun sets and darkness descends.

Suddenly I heard the sound of a human voice, a man singing. He was not far off, though the sound easily carried throughout the woods. I assume that he thought that no one was near enough to hear him. It was Pablo, one of our monks. He was singing a hymn to Mary in Spanish in his deep, rich voice, which, on that evening, was more beautiful than ever. His words left his heart and moved through the woods as if looking for the woman he sang to that night with such tenderness and love.

For an instant, Pablo's voice blended with all the other sounds of that evening. There was no separation from the songs of the birds, the gentle rustling of the leaves, the laughter of a nearby creek. It all comprised a single evening song, a song of all that is lovely and forever and unseen. It was as if every living creature around me shared in the very heart of being, the heart of God, who gives voice to both singing monks and chirping birds.

Be alone somewhere and listen to that song.

Late
Afternoon
Light

It was late afternoon, and the rays of the setting sun shone through the stained-glass windows of the monastery church, coloring the walls and floor with beautiful pastel colors. Blues, greens, reds and yellows rested and blended with ease on the tall white concrete walls. The wooden choir stalls looked as if they had been adorned for an evening out on the town. They basked in a dazzling array of color.

I sat near the front, not far from the altar of reposition where the Eucharist is kept. I had the church to myself. The day's work was done, and it would be another half-hour before the rest of the monks came into the church for Vespers.

Gazing at the burning candle near the tabernacle, I wondered about the meaning of the true presence of the risen and glorified Christ, made so through the consecration of bread and wine.

One of our monks walked in. He caught my eye as he walked into the church from the cloister and gently smiled at me and slowly continued his way across the front of the church. The sunlight noticed him, too, and played on his habit as he walked. He stopped before the Blessed Sacrament, bowed very low, then straightened up and continued on his way to his place in choir, far behind where I was sitting that afternoon.

I could feel his presence in the church. His sitting behind me transformed the atmosphere. I felt especially close to him, and allowed his presence to touch me as deeply as I could. I prayed for him, for his well-being, for whatever hopes he harbored in his heart that day. Yet I knew that I would never tell him any of that.

The monastery is a place where, among other things, one comes to terms with oneself in solitude. One must also, however, come to terms with others. A monastic enclosure invites you to live essentially—with only the very basics of human, and therefore social, existence. There are not many things that we monks do for one another. We do not exchange gifts, for example. Ours is not a competitive life; there are no career tracks, no special hats to wear. And so there is a minimum of ulterior motives regarding human relationships. You cannot use another man to get someplace or to secure something other than simply being a friend.

In the quiet of that church that afternoon, amid the play of light on the walls, I prayed. There is a light in each of us, a light that is somehow in everything and in everyone. It attracts, warms otherwise cold and lifeless words and actions, and offers a context for beauty, truth, and desire. It illumines parameters for restraint, limits, and silence. It offers a way of discernment, of simply knowing that we are not the masters of our origins or ultimate destinies. The light can catch us unaware and leave us to give pause and marvel at its loveliness . . . and encourage a smile, a bow and a slow walk in silence.

In the fading light of a late afternoon, I saw a monk who gave his life to a God no one of us truly knows.

Who are you, Lord Jesus? Your presence and our lives are inseparable. We, too, are living tabernacles, upon whom your light shines. We cannot understand a Eucharistic presence apart from your presence everywhere.

My friend, my brother, smiled at me and bent his body before you. I smiled back and prayed.

Spider Webs

Personal space, a bit of land, a home, a soft living-room chair before a fireplace, a winter's scene outside the window, a book in one's lap, all blending together to make for a near-perfect American dream. Sigh.

I confess that I have wanted such, but have only been able to get bits and pieces of it. When I entered the Monastery of the Holy Spirit, however, I had to divest myself of even those. I left the fireplace behind. The books I donated to a library. Most of the other things I gave to friends. Can't have much here in a monastery—there is simply no room for it.

I never really had a home of my own, though the thought of having one is something that still crosses my mind: a nice little fence and mailbox; neighbors who wave hello as they walk their doggies; the paper boy or girl, wearing a baseball cap and riding a red bike, shouting a friendly "Hi, Mr. Behrens!" as the *Evening Star* is tossed across my well-kept lawn; frosted windows on a wintry morn; little neighborhood kids coming by dressed as witches, ghosts and goblins on Halloween, giggling at ol' friendly Mr. B., as I would surely be known. The sound of a train whistle in the distance would be a nice touch.

I would answer the door wearing my favorite old sweater with a pipe in my mouth. My wife, June, would be at my side, smiling at the little ones. Our dog, Ruff, would bark just a bit, raising his head off the parquet floor.

Are Tommy Hilfiger sweaters still in?

Oh, well.

I sat on the retreat house porch every morning for about two weeks when I first came here. There were several rounds of interviews I had to go through before I was notified of my acceptance into the community. I had left a lot of stuff in New Jersey, and I worried about it constantly during those weeks. I eventually did go through a minor version of hell getting rid of it all, and it took me a while to feel good about it. Now it is all gone, except for a few mementos I am glad I kept.

On the porch every morning I had coffee and a few cigarettes and looked out over a beautifully kept garden. One morning I noticed the spider webs. I suppose that they were there every morning, but I did not notice them right away. There would usually be two or three stretched between the porch and some nearby trees. The webs were huge, about two to four feet across. The spiders were not all that big. But they sure could weave. They were dwarfed by their own creations. I sat transfixed at the intricate patterns of the webs—tiny rectangular shapes, hundreds of them, all connected to form a precise circle. The dew made them glisten and added an extra touch of beauty.

One morning I went out later than usual, just to look at the webs, and they were all gone. I could not imagine what had happened. Maybe they had some substance that made them dry up easily? Or had someone knocked them down? Was the wind the culprit? Or one of the monks? I was intrigued.

So, the next morning I went out earlier, and the webs spun during the night were there. All new ones. I sat down with my coffee and ciga- rette and waited and watched. The sun rose higher, and soon enough I had my answer.

One by one, the spiders somehow ingested their own webs. I am not sure whether that is the right word. But I saw them put their webs into some orifice as they very patiently moved across and up and down them—an amazing sight. The webs gradually vanished.

I thought a lot about myself, watching those spiders that morning and several mornings thereafter.

There I was, worrying about the once-in-a-lifetime move I was about to make, and here were these creatures who had to go through such travail every morning of their lives. Imagine having to cram your house and all your belongings into yourself every morning? And then rebuild it every night? And rebuild it perfectly? I laughed at myself.

Pity the poor spider, who has no home to call its own.

Pity those of us who do and are stuck with it and all our stuff.

The Man
Who Laughed
with the Rain

Just at the bottom of a fairly steep path that winds down toward the lakes behind the monastery buildings is a large shed. It is used to store some old machinery. There are a few buckets and a large wooden barrel. It is a good place to read. I can sit on the barrel and read for several hours, taking in the peace around me. On a hot day, the shade cools things off a bit. On a windy day, the shed affords some shelter from the wind. And on rainy days, the shed keeps my book and me dry.

There was a young man at Mass this morning. He was in a wheelchair. He wheeled himself into the monastery church and took a spot near the sanctuary steps. He appears to be in his late twenties and severely crippled with muscular dystrophy. I recognized him from earlier visits. He waved to the monks as they processed in for Mass, and several of the monks went over to greet him. He looked up at them and smiled, raising his arms and waving, elated that he was personally welcomed. I greeted him as I later walked up the stairs to the sanctuary, and he extended his hand to me. He had difficulty grasping my hand, so I simply took his in mine and we shook. He smiled.

He went his way after Mass, back to the retreat house where he was staying. I busied myself the rest of the day, not thinking about the young man at all.

I was in the shed later that night reading a novel. I found it hard to get into the book. My mind was still racing from some scattered and insignificant events of the day. Morning Mass seemed like ages ago.

The day had been full. I had to take out the garbage, run some things off on the copier, do my laundry, and finish up some other odds and ends that I usually leave to the weekend. The book stayed open in my lap, and I gazed around me. I brushed away an occasional mosquito or a restless wasp. Some little birds flew into the shed and made straight for a pile of sand. There were three of them, and they found a spot in the sand, wiggled around as if cleaning themselves, flew away, and then returned to the same spot and did the same thing. Several deer grazed lazily not too far down the road, oblivious to my presence. The geese and ducks made their occasional racket down near the lake. I just sat there taking it all in.

Clouds were gathering. I looked up and saw diminishing patches of blue. The first drops of rain surprised me, since the skies were not all that ominous. The rain tapped the tin roof of the shed, falling lightly and evenly. Then I heard thunder, and the sky did begin to darken. Storms can arrive in Conyers in a matter of minutes. I looked at my watch and grew anxious that I would get caught in the rain and not be able to make it back on time for night prayers.

The even cadence of the drops swelled to a roar as gallons of rain pelted the tin roof of the shed.

Movement on the road caught my eye. Someone was pushing the young fellow from Mass in the wheelchair. They could not see me. Suddenly, they stopped, both drenched. The man in the wheelchair raised his arms to the heavens, his face broke into a smile, and he started to laugh. He waved his arms, as if welcoming some unseen presence that lived in the rain. This went on for a few seconds and then the two proceeded on their way back up the hill to the monastery, to the warmth and shelter of the buildings.

Seeing this man welcome the rain yanked me right out of my own little world. There I was, in my sheltered shed, worrying about getting wet, when an angel on wheels arrived, a friend to misfortune, to laugh and wave his weakened arms in ecstasy.

Long ago, I read that only Revelation can reveal Revelation. The One who reveals must speak. I have read the Book of Revelation, have said a lot of fancy things about it, and can quote chapter and verse. But I cannot say that the One who spoke was revealed to me—until tonight.

Tonight, the veil parted just a bit. I pray that I now know just a little something of the reality of God.

The Kitten
in the Dumpster

Not long ago I had to haul a heap of garbage to a green metal dumpster that is parked behind the retreat house. Just as I was about to empty the contents of a large garbage can into the dumpster, I heard a muffled cry and then a "meow" coming from the depths of the huge bin. I looked over the edge and scanned every nook and cranny of refuse, but I could not see the kitten. I knew it was there, however, for I soon heard the shifting sounds of garbage and saw a small mound of paper and trash in the corner move.

Mike, a layman who is the retreat house cook, saw me from the window and knew that something was amiss. He came outside and asked if he could help in any way. Then Karen, a frequent guest at the monastery, came from the kitchen. Karen is in the military, and without further ado she climbed into the dumpster and foraged through the rubbish for the kitten. She found it, and it scampered from one end of the dumpster to the other. It was a cute gray kitten, only a few weeks old. I was amazed how such a little creature possessed such dexterity.

Karen leaped across the goo and lunged for the kitten and succeeded in grabbing him. Once lifted from the rubbish, the kitten began to cry and scratch and bite Karen's hands. I suppose that he thought himself to be in even more of a predicament than being trapped in a dumpster. I am quite sure that Karen's hands were his first contact with humans, a species he had carefully avoided thus far in his young life.

Mike threw a towel to Karen, and she carefully wrapped the kitten and tried to soothe him with soft words. She held the bundle close to her body, and he soon calmed down and just stared at his captor, his eyes wide and very frightened. Karen climbed out of the dumpster and freed our little friend. He scampered off into the woods, stopping at the tree line, looking back at us for a few seconds, and then running off into the shelter of the trees. I am sure that I will see him again very soon, but am also sure that he will avoid that dumpster for the rest of his life.

How strange and frightening we humans must seem to other creatures, especially when they fear that we will harm them.

Later, I thought about God and humans. Here we are, trapped in this walled expanse of life, a place we try to dress up as much as possible. Fear of loss makes us do terrible things to ourselves and to each other. Those of us who live fairly peaceful lives know well that there are other areas that gnaw at the fringes of our composure. Our peace is relative, provisional, fragile—often lived at a terrible expense to others. We do not yet share this walled existence very well.

Grace abounds in the world. Like Karen with the kitten, God has reached into the dumpster that is the world and then climbed in and stayed. That presence has made love stronger than fear. It is a love that can and will outrun our most feverish attempts to flee.

Maybe that little kitten had a second thought looking back in that instant before he dashed to his freedom in the woods. Maybe he sensed that we humans are not so bad after all. Neither, perhaps, is God.

Edmund's Eyes

Edmund is one of the senior monks at the Monastery of the Holy Spirit. The way he walks, smiles, listens, speaks all emanates from a deep and gentle way that is simply Edmund.

One night it was Edmund's turn to read the closing prayer at Compline, the seventh and last prayer of the day. He moved in the darkened church to the lectern and slowly opened the book of prayers. We could hear the pages turn as he tried to find the right spot. After about two minutes, he raised his head and spoke into the darkness. "I cannot see," he said softly. And then again, louder, "I cannot see."

Immediately, another monk, Joseph, came to the rescue, and as Edmund stepped to the side the prayer was read. Edmund bowed his head and prayed with the rest of us. Afterward we left the church as we do every night, as one body in a single file, bowing before the Abbot for his blessing and then heading upstairs to bed and sleep.

I am theoretically aware that we are one body here. I know the theology behind it and the long tradition of Christian sources that support the notion of oneness among many members. That night when Edmund said that he could not see, however, I experienced how he was literally given eyes by Joseph and how the rest of us were given a sense of what we can and do mean to one another.

I have so often seen here a lived and deep sense of shared life, of a truly common body. It is as commonplace as the air we breathe. The strong members of the community give freely to the weaker ones, and the weak ones give the strong a living example of the gentleness and wisdom that comes with accepting human limitations.

Some day, I hope to see as Edmund sees.

Signs of Life

Many months ago, my sister Mary brought a small tree that belongs to a friend of hers to our bonsai shop at the monastery. The tree was in very bad shape, withered and brown, with hardly a trace of life to it.

One of our monks, who is a bonsai expert, examined the tree carefully. He sees life and its wondrous possibilities in all things. This monk chooses to remain anonymous. But if you ever come here and bring with you an ailing plant (or heart), he will rise with joy from his obscurity. He always does when someone is in need.

He gently teased the soil at the base of the trunk and with a cry of delight found the tiniest green leaf sprouting just at the soil line. "Yes, yes," he said, as if he had just discovered gold, "This tree will be fine."

I was amazed. I never would have given the little tree a chance. It turns out that the tree was a wedding anniversary gift that a friend of Mary's had given to his wife, and she apparently lacked a green bonsai thumb.

The tree is now taller, full of leaves, healthy branches and new growth. It has grown to twice the size it was when Mary first brought it. All this has come from that tiny speck of green and a monk's vigilant and tender care.

I like to think that our lives are sometimes like that tree. We may look at ourselves and all we may see are dead ends, withered possibilities, shrunken prospects and dried and shriveled hopes. But at the bottom of such decay may well be the tiniest movement of life. It is from that mere point that we should pray.

Plants need time and patience to develop and grow. We can easily give them that. What is more difficult is giving our weaknesses over to God and allowing God to love us just as we are. All growth, like that little tree, starts from the smallest possibilities and spreads upward and outward to genuine sources of life. Human life is no different. Our deepest hunger is for God, who is our light, our sustenance, our very food.

A Change of Beat

One of the first monks I met here was Brother William. He worked and lived in the retreat house where I stayed for two weeks during the initial interview process before entering the monastery. I would get up earlier than I had to and write or read in the retreat house dining room. William was always there ahead of me, making the coffee and readying the place for the day's guests.

During that time William told me a few things about himself. He was a Franciscan and served in Peru before entering the Trappists. He grew up in New Jersey, as did I. And he plays the saxophone. He told me that he played in clubs all over the New York metropolitan area and astounded me when he said that he played clubs in Newark. I told him that must have been before my time.

I found out later that William put away his saxophone when he entered religious life. I sense, though he never told me, that the instrument represented for him a way of life, even perhaps a way of love, that he freely chose to leave behind when he became a monk. Looking at him sing in choir, I can tell that he loves music. He walks in measured steps, and there is something harmonious about the way he is so open and friendly with people.

I suppose that any life choice demands a parting of ways, a series of sacrifices that must be made if we are to move ahead and follow our heart's true desire. Any given day is filled with such choices. Things are done and even said at the expense of other, equally good, things.

I like to observe William's joy and real zest as he goes through his days here. His affection for life is contagious. At this point, it can be said that he chose to follow the call of a different drum and attuned his heart to a new song.

In the process of doing so, I do not think that he has ever missed a beat.

The Pathmaker

Early Christianity was called the Way, and we are called to follow it and to help others do the same.

To walk the Way is to walk in goodness. It is to live your life for others. Yet we can easily get lost until a fellow traveler helps us along.

There are large wooded areas at the monastery where people rarely venture. The floor of the forest is hidden beneath a deep layer of leaves, brush and pine needles. In some areas, the only paths are those that have been worn and made firm by the many deer who feel much at home here.

One day, I was walking in such an area and up ahead of me I saw movement. It was Gerard, one of our monks, walking through the forest. He did not see me, and I did not want to startle him. I slowed a bit and then noticed that he was dragging something behind him. It looked to be some sort of heavy mat that had a rope attached to it. He was stooped as he slowly moved ahead of me.

Gerard spotted me and then smiled and stopped, waiting for me to catch up to him. As I approached him, I saw that the mat was actually made of a metal mesh. I asked him if he wanted me to carry it for a while and he said no, that he was making a path through the woods. And sure enough, I saw that where he had dragged the mat, there was a leveling of the grass and the leaves. "Others may want to walk here," he said. "This will make it easier." And that was that. We chatted for a while, and then went our separate ways. I headed back to the monastery buildings, and Gerard advanced into the woods, dragging his little pathmaker behind him.

Henry James, when asked what three things he felt to be the necessary qualities for a good and full life, responded by saying, "The first is kindness, and the second is kindness, and the third is kindness." I do not think Gerard has ever had to think much about choosing any other options. Everything he does has a genuine touch of kindness to it, from his smile, to his concern for others, to the way he walks.

Every now and then while walking in the forest, I come across a path that seems to have been laid down before me by magic. Then I think of Gerard, moving gently through the woods, making a path for others. I do not think that he ever told anyone else what he does, but a lot can be learned from just watching a man like him.

Calling My Name

We have a house here at the monastery reserved for the families and friends of the monks. It is an old, beautiful house situated on a lake and has all the comforts of home. Our families and friends come from far and wide and stay for several days, and those days are always filled with catching up on family news and above all the joy of simply being with family.

Departures, however, are always difficult for me. My mom, sister and brothers live great distances from here, and saying good-by is always a heavyhearted experience.

After one such departure, I needed time alone and went back into the empty guest house. I sat in a large comfortable rocking chair and turned on the television set. We normally do not watch TV in the cloister, and it felt strange listening to disembodied voices and perfectly timed sound and laughter. There was a comedy on and in my empty-hearted state the routines seemed canned and predictable. I was lonely and missed the presence of others, but I did not want to leave just then to go looking for someone back at the main building. I still needed time to savor the fresh and lingering love and presence of my family.

Suddenly I heard a knock at the back door and then heard it open and my name called. I immediately recognized the voice as Mark's, one of our monks. The simple call of my name from a friend was in sharp contrast to the anonymous sound emanating from the television. Mark's voice gave me a deep sense of being called back to myself and to the world of friendship, care and commitment to one another that is our community.

I called to Mark to come in, and he entered the room with a warm smile and sat in a chair next to me. He said that he had driven down to the main gate and said good-by to my family. I was touched by his thoughtfulness and told him so. I was equally moved by his returning to the guest house, where he seemed to know I would be—and in need of friendship. The hour or so that we spent talking that night had a sacred quality to it—two solitudes that touched in a way that needed no explanation to verify it.

When Mark called my name, I awoke once again to the goodness of my life here. I had a profound sense that night that I never really said good-by to the best of what my family is about. In the person of Mark and those like him, I know I have here in the monastery what is most real about my family. We seek one another with a love and presence that is more genuine than the entire world of mass media and high-tech communication.

Nature's Course

I had been working right near the tree for several weeks, and I did not see the nest. It was small, hardly noticeable. It could have easily fit in a human hand. What brought my attention to it was the sound of baby birds chirping. Careful not to disturb them, I moved close to the tree and was surprised that the nest had been built at eye level. Had I wanted to, I could have easily reached in and touched the baby birds.

As I stood there, the mother bird hesitated to return to the nest. She monitored my movement from a telephone wire a stone's throw away. Only after I moved what she considered a safe distance away did she fly to the nest and feed her young. I counted four little chicks, their tiny fuzzy heads frantically bobbing up and down as soon as they sensed that their mother was near.

I returned to the area near the tree each day for several weeks after discovering the small brood and was fascinated by the vigilant care the mother lavished on the four baby birds. She made constant trips back and forth to the nest, returning each time with morsels of food.

The chicks grew rapidly. By simply watching the routine of their mother I picked up some small lessons in nature and nurture that I had never known. The mother would not come to the nest if I stood nearby, and if I drew too close she would chirp wildly. Not wanting to cause any undue alarm, I would gently back off, freeing her from worry. I also noticed that the chicks instinctively grew quiet, and even cowered to the bottom of the nest, when I drew close.

One morning, I approached the nest and was startled to see that it was empty. By then I well knew the distinctive sound of the young birds, and I soon heard, from several directions not at all far from me, their plaintive chirps. I stepped back and kept myself at a safe distance, just waiting to see what would transpire.

It was not long before I realized what had happened. The young had simply reached a point in their development when they could venture on their own from the nest. I was able to see all four of them, in various branches hopping distances away from the nest. One young chick, however, had fallen and was chirping wildly from a handful of brush not far from where I was standing. Fearing that it would soon fall prey to one of the cats that frequented the area, I moved toward it and gingerly grasped the little bird, but as soon as I took it into my hands both the baby and its mother began to chirp frantically. I knew immediately that I had overstepped a natural boundary, so I placed the small creature on the ground. It hobbled off toward the nearest shelter it could find, which happened to be the base of an enormous tree. The other three chicks were silent, and as I got far enough away the mother bird flew to her wandering chick and fed it.

Things seemed to go well for the rest of that day, though I noticed that the chick that I had picked up was in an orbit of its own, seemingly unable to get back to the safer refuge of its siblings, who had kept to the branches of the tree where they were born.

The next day, the young chick was not to be found. The other three were still safe in the tree, and I watched their mother make numerous flights back and forth to them. Not once did I see her stray from her trips to that tree. I never again was able to account for the missing and almost surely dead bird. I looked for it and never found a trace of it. As the weeks passed, I watched the brood brave ever-widening horizons, their mother continuing to feed them all the while. One day, however, they must have reached a point where they were able to fend for themselves, since all that was left of their lives was an empty nest.

How I wish I had not interfered with nature's course. Perhaps that little bird would have somehow made it to where its siblings now fly with abandon. It may seem like a paltry thing for me to fret over, since nature is, I know, harsh to begin with. But my reaching out that morning seemed to seal the fate of a creature so small, innocent and dependent.

Thinking of life writ large, I realize that being human invariably involves so many decisions, indeed, so many risks—and that many of these risks can involve loss. Perhaps love is the most intricate and most exacting of these risks. When we give from our deepest self there are no sure maps and no guarantees as to how it will all turn out.

Perhaps my tale of the little bird is too simple and worthy of dismissal. But I believe that seemingly small things bear within them the capacity to teach lessons of great magnitude. I can only ask forgiveness from what slips through my hand and be grateful for whatever I may help along the way.

At times it is difficult to be vigilant and tender toward all that is small and seemingly insignificant, yet life abounds with such things. Perhaps their plenitude exists because we are so slow to learn.

On Watering Plants

One summer, I was assigned to water plants each day, four hours a day, for just over four months. I worried a lot about keeping my mind active as I watched umpteen gallons of water splash over the plants. I sang songs to myself, mused over my past, thought about my plans for the future, tried hard to take my task one day at a time. I was trying to think my way into meaningfulness.

I thought about people all over the world who were doing more relevant, and obviously more successful things, than I. In many ways, I felt that I was wasting time, that there were surely more important things that I could be doing with my life.

I felt like a human siphon. Water was passing through me and not much else. I experienced very little fulfillment or genuine pleasure. I was watering plants, period. What's more, people looked at me and did not even wave or otherwise acknowledge my existence. Something about that particular job smeared me onto the canvas of oblivion.

I never got angry at the plants. It was not their fault. As a matter of fact, I soon began to take to heart the fact that they somehow needed me. I soon found myself talking to them, worrying about them, checking each of them for signs of illness and fatigue. I wondered if they possessed any sort of consciousness—if they ever grew jealous when their neighbors received more water or a better place in the sun. I wondered if they felt sadness as they lost their leaves or even their lives. All these things wandered through my mind as I carefully aimed the hose and allowed the clear and cool water to gush, splash, squirt and spray.

Each plant required a different method of water allocation and delivery. I learned this as time went on. I also watched for soil levels and whether fertilizer was needed. I looked out for harmful bugs and worms. I soon knew the difference between good bugs and not-so-good bugs. There were many little tricks that I picked up as the days grew into weeks and then months. I fancied myself something of a watering expert by summer's end—no diploma, no certificate, no added line on my curriculum vita, but an expert just the same.

And something good did come out of it.

That something has to do with the human need to engage in seemingly useless activity . . .

and to do so on purpose. It concerns doing things without a hope of getting something back. I now realize that such activity is how life itself thrives and blooms.

We have to keep an eye open for where such activity occurs, however, for it is almost invisible. It blends in with the scenery as it goes about tending to its daily tasks.

Just as the monastery plants would have died without the water I delivered, we, too, would die without all that gushes continuously around us: goodness, patience, kindness, hope, human warmth—given so freely by so many, usually with little or no notice.

Threads of Grace

I went for a walk earlier this morning in the monastery woods. It was a cool day and this morning was particularly beautiful. The sun shone through the hundreds of trees in the forest, and countless spider webs glistened, strewn between branches no matter where I looked. It was as if thousands of fairies had been busy throughout the night, stringing strands of precious silver thread from branch to branch, for no other reason than to add more beauty for me to observe.

As the sun rose, however, the strands vanished from sight. The delicate threads need the bright rays of morning for visibility.

I think of grace as spider webs that are always present in our lives. Every so often—say in a brilliant and clear moment like this morning—we can see how beautiful everything is, connected by glistening strands, dancing and swaying all around us. With less light, the grace remains, but we have to look a bit harder for it.

And in the times of total darkness, we must make an act of faith that grace still abounds.

Cat Greetings

His name is BC, short for Barn Cat. We found him as a kitten, and he has made the large bonsai barn his home. He is orange and with his winter coat looks fat and fluffy.

Walking down to the barn yesterday morning, I was whistling some forgettable tune to myself. Out of the corner of my eye I saw movement, and there was BC bouncing across the field toward me. He was meowing as he trotted along, glad to see a familiar face after a long and perhaps lonesome night in the field, though he prefers it out there and has found a way to exit the barn whenever he feels a pang of hunger or wanderlust (or maybe just plain old lust).

BC came right up to me and brushed against my legs. I leaned over and petted him and was happy to see him. I thought how such a mundane little ritual as a cat greeting a man can lift one's spirits. I realized that much of creation greets us daily. There is a welcoming sense to nature, despite its occasional harshness and in-difference to those who are passing through.

Maybe there is something to learn from the gentle brush of a cat or a branch or a breeze.

BC was glad to see me. It is as simple as that. I made it a point to remember to express the same gratitude to those who crossed my path that day.

The Monastic Vocation

Vaun was a teacher of socially disadvantaged kids before he entered the Monastery of the Holy Spirit. His religious name here is Chaminade.

I like to hear Chaminade talk of his teaching experience. He speaks with fondness of the kids he knew over the years and still worries about them. He wanted them to have a chance at a good and better life and knew the importance of education. I sense that he must have been a wonderful presence in a classroom. He is a very open person, warmly attracted and attractive to others.

Diversity does not seem to bother Chaminade. He moves easily through difference, not trying to reduce it to a singularity of any sort. In his quiet way, he allows people to be themselves. Perhaps that is why I find him such a pleasure to be with.

We wrap pots together in our bonsai department and have the chance to talk a lot as we select pots and prepare them for shipment. As the pots are wrapped in plastic bubble wrap and placed in boxes, our conversation touches upon all sorts of things. I like to get Chaminade laughing—he has a good laugh, a laugh that comes from deep inside of him, from that place where his students still live and claim his concern.

One day, he told me how much he misses teaching. He has mentioned this before, but on that particular day he seemed especially worried and sad. It is a struggle for most monks, wondering if we would be doing some more tangible good elsewhere—in Chaminade's case back in a classroom.

That was the question he was posing and for which I have no easy or sure answer. Can one remain in a cloistered monastery and serve by simply being what one feels called to be? Chaminade imparts something to everyone with his smile, his integrity, his fidelity to seeking truthfulness. Is he not a teacher? Does teaching necessarily involve a building and classrooms, a student body and faculty, taxes and tuition? Or is the essence of teaching the learned and the unlearned, with some sense of reciprocity between the two?

I looked at Chaminade. I know that he teaches by all that he is. He teaches of the God who loves him and somehow has beckoned him to this monastic life—to wonder, to seek, to re-fine and to share who he is and what he knows.

A friend once gave me a chalice on which is engraved: "You give much and know not at all that you give." I think that the words are those of Kahlil Gibran. We never know much about how others see us; what it is that we give to them. I doubt that it is of any matter to see ourselves as others do. Maybe in God's plan it is more impor-tant to see what others give, what their lives teach us.

Maybe that is the secret of the monastic vocation.

The Art
of Wasting Time

Our culture thrives on doing. Idle time is easily seen as nonproductive. Many people experience guilt if they find that they have time on their hands and cannot fill it with something. I have often thought how youngsters these days are so caught up in an adolescent version of the rat race, having their days so compartmentalized. Everything is planned for them. Much of the spontaneity and frivolity that should be part and parcel of "play" has been neatly ordered and packaged by well-intentioned adults whose own lives are burdened by all sorts of schedules and routines.

I suggest that we all learn the art of wasting time. But please, don't plan it. Just do it.

I used to like sitting on the front steps of my home in the evening during the warm summer months. I sat there and listened and watched and wondered. I liked the sounds of laughter, of people talking, of a late-afternoon breeze as it caressed the trees. I liked to watch the passing cars, and every so often the evening was graced with the beauty of a full and rich moon, with clouds chasing each other across the sky's surface. I looked at the stars and contemplated their beauty and unimaginable distance. I may have been wasting time, but I do not regret it.

In the stillness of many a summer night, the memory of that street where I lived and the heavens above me become one, and I am where they meet.

What, then, do monks do? Some say that we do nothing. Absolutely nothing.

Others say that in doing so, we are involved in absolutely everything.

There is a great porch at the rear of our monastery church. I go there on summer nights and sit and do nothing. The shooting stars above Conyers are a glory to behold. There is always an extra chair.

Conyers Spring

We had a glorious spring this year. There were many cool days, which brought with them a good balance of sun and rain. So much comes to life in the spring: the trees, new plants, the grasses and shrubs, and of course all the animals. And here in the South, the night air is filled with the sounds of millions of insects. By early summer, baby birds, deer, kittens and squirrels are plentiful. This spring I had the joy of watching on many a morning as a mama turkey and her eight plump chicks fed near the forest's edge behind the barn where I read.

All the above is just what one monk sees and hears. I can only imagine all the life around me that I cannot see, yet I know it teems there. Spring springs to life all on its own. As a Zen master once said, "Sit back and the spring comes."

The earth renews itself through its seasonal cycles in ways that we are only beginning to fathom. The earth is a living system—it heals, renews, balances and replenishes; it dies and rises again.

We humans are a living part of this mystery. We, too, have seasons of decline and renewal, times that are spiritually lean and times of abundant harvest.

To behold a spring day in Conyers is indeed wonderful. To entrust my life to the God who creates such beauty here is a privilege.

Note by Note

Being a cantor in a monastic choir can be a humbling lesson in getting lost and being found. There are many things to learn when one starts out as a novice in the *schola* here—the proper notes, cadence, and page numbers; who does which response when; when to sing and when to remain silent. These things must be remembered all at once, and it can get unnerving to say the least.

I have floundered many times. What both amazed and heartened me were my fellow monks, who bailed me out and kept the chant going as smoothly as if nothing had happened. I soon learned that there is an instinctive willingness among the monks to pitch in and retrieve a wandering or lost note (or novice). It took me a good while to trust that larger sense of organic care that exists in the choir and, as I have learned, all through the life here. My realization of its presence grew in proportion to my need for it. We monks strive to live (and sing) for God and one another. Where one monk may be weak, the strength or charity of another finds what is lost or wayward and cares for that loss by love, prayer, or the right and perfectly timed note.

Being a human gathering, a monastery is far from a perfect system. We do not make up a perfect body, but that does not matter. Perfection is not what monastic life is about. On more than one occasion, when my notes (or my charity) have gone flat and sour, I have been sung or simply loved right back into the music of the life here.

Learning the Ropes

One of my daily jobs in the monastery is the ringing of the church bells for the Angelus and Compline. It may sound like an easy enough job, but I found out the first time I did it that it would take me more than a few times to get it right. There is an art to pulling the long rope just right and doing it at the required pace and with the proper amount of yank.

My first few days at the task were rocky. My timing was way off and in my nervousness I pulled the rope an extra time or two. The bell also tolled flat. For ten days thereafter, one of the veteran monks stood right in front of me as I tolled the bell, coaching me and encouraging me. With his help and patience, I graduated to solo and the bells now ring loud and clear. Eventually, I will be showing someone else the ropes.

One discovers oneself through the delight of learning to love and be loved. Teachers abound—those gifted and generous people who love well and teach us to ring the symphonies of our own bells. The learning is in the doing and persisting—through days and sometimes years— until loving is as easy and as natural as ringing a bell.

The Heart of Texas

I was in Texas once, many years ago, for the wedding of a friend. I did not see much of the state, certainly nowhere near what I needed to get a feel for the place.

I was recently given a taste of Texas once again, however, and I got there through a song.

Not long ago, Brother Tom, our cantor, invited me down to the monastery guest house to spend the evening with his sister Mary and their dad, Al. They were here for a few days from San Antonio. They are the kind of people who welcome you into their lives with ease and warmth. After just a little while with them, I felt that I had known them all my life.

We sat around the kitchen table, relaxing and sharing stories. The sun had gone down, but I could still see some ducks gliding softly across the lake just outside the window of the kitchen. Mary, in the course of the conversation, asked

Tom if he remembered a particular song that they used to sing together as kids. Tom slowly sang the first few verses of a Burl Ives song that I had never heard before. Tom has a beautiful voice, and Mary and Al smiled as they joined in. Mary asked Tom if he remembered one other song, and then another, and another. She recalled snatches of lyrics and a bit of melody, and Tom was able to immediately offer the rest of the song. In between the songs, the three of them laughed and reminisced about the circumstances surrounding each song. It was as if each tune were a line thrown into a sea of memory that pulled a story of their lives to the surface—warm and glistening and very much alive.

A few of songs were about Texas. All of them were about love and hope and loss.

Texas will always be a place I visited that night in a Georgia kitchen. I was asked to go there, and indeed I went. Tom's family's easy ways gave me a glimpse of the vastness and wealth of Texas and the warmth of its people. What I saw of Texas that night I loved. It is a wonder to me how a place so big can fit so easily in a human heart and be shared so fully in a matter of hours.

Now I do not have to travel to get to Texas. When Tom sings in the choir, I listen to him and am easily carried back again to that night in the kitchen . . . and from there to Texas. The cloister makes such travel possible. It is not so much a place as a state of mind.

Sacred Graves

It lies hidden in the woods, not far off a path that winds its way through the forest that surrounds the monastery. The woods are in the monastic enclosure, so we monks are the only ones who wander through it these days. We seem to be the only ones who know where the cemetery is.

One of the older monks told me about it and showed me the way. I have gone there by myself many times to pray.

It is a slave cemetery.

It is a sacred place, a hollowed place. The remains of the slaves lie buried beneath the forest, the ground covered with leaves and rocks and dead branches. The only things that mark the graves as such are small, rough stones that look as if they were just thrown about. You have to observe carefully to discern that they have a pattern and that the earth before each stone is

117

slightly sunken. There are no crosses or legible markers of any kind. The graves have been untouched and largely unknown, except by the monks, for more than one hundred years.

I walked down there on Good Friday and thought of the lives whose remains lay beneath me, forever lost to history and human memory. I prayed to the God who cried and sweat and suffered with them, to the same God whose Son died and lay buried in an unmarked, borrowed grave.

The woods are silent, save for the sound of the wind, the songs of the birds, the hum and cadence of the insects.

I pray that I learn to hear the silent cries of those who lie there in peace, in the womb of an earth that has been seeded with the life of the One who shall call them to rise again.

One Hand Reaching Out to Another

One month after my father passed away, I preached at a Memorial Mass celebrated for him at the monastery. It was a very hard thing for me to do, and I considered ducking the invitation. I wanted to share with my fellow monks some thoughts about Dad, a man I loved very much whom they had never met. But the pain of losing him was still deep and fresh, and I did not want to get overly emotional.

Toward the end of the homily, the combination of my love for my father and the love I have been so freely given by the monks here at Conyers welled up in my heart. I stared at the few notes I had and started to cry. I had reached that place where there is only wordless mystery. I bowed my head, folded my notes, and proceeded slowly back to my place in the choir. As I passed Abbot Bernard, I felt his hand reach out and take mine and gently squeeze it.

Emmanuel means "God with us." I do not believe that God exists apart from our need to reach out and touch those spaces that ache in each other. There is no "God not with us."

Dom Bernard grasped my hand in human solidarity, and as I sat down I remembered what I tearfully told Dad as he lay dying and asked me what I thought would happen to him. I told him to try to be at peace and pray that God would take him by the hand and bring him to his eternal home.

Emmanuel, our joy and our very life, we pray that you give us the hope that is your presence. Help us to reach out to each other with our hands . . . and our hearts.

Karen's Resolution

Being organized is not a strong trait of mine. I have tried many times to become a more disciplined person, but I have as many times lapsed back into the same old routines. Paperwork piles up. Jobs take on a scattered quality. I plan one thing and end up doing something else. I make lists and misplace them. I even bought a book on how to stop procrastinating and put off reading it.

I was in a bit of a funk not too long ago about all this as I walked down to the bonsai barn, where we store all our bonsai pots for shipment. Karen, who works there, greeted me cheerily as I walked in.

Karen champions the bright side of things. She paid me a few kind words that so lifted my spirits that I once again made myself a promise to organize myself just a little bit better.

For a modest start, I promised to write a little

bit each day, no matter how I felt, and to make one list of ten things to get done.

This resolution has helped a lot. I am writing each day and have only two more things to accomplish on my list. Item nine is to make a new list and item ten is to write this little essay on Karen's kind words. Ten has been a joy.

Number nine I'll do later.

Anne's Kittens

The voice was so soft I barely heard it. It took a while for me to discern where it was coming from as I moved slowly in its direction. It was a late-summer evening and I was walking on the road behind our retreat house. In the light coming from the back of the retreat house porch I saw her. It was Anne, who works and lives in the retreat house. I could see her on the porch, leaning over just a bit, but she did not see me.

I kept walking slowly, not wanting to frighten or disturb her. Then I saw movement at her feet. I counted three kittens, inching their way toward her, being enticed by the soothing quality of her voice. She had set out a dish of leftovers and was trying to win them over. Finally, she looked up and saw me, smiled and waved. I waved back and continued on my way.

I, too, felt soothed and assured by Anne's voice that night. I know her to be a kind and caring woman, and I was moved by her solitude that night. She was alone, but she was calling to the kittens to befriend them and share her goodness with them.

We assume that humans are the only ones who truly hear and speak. True, our hearing and speaking are different from other creatures, and some say that we are of a higher order because of such faculties. But that night I heard around me myriad sounds—crickets and frogs, ducks and geese, owls, dogs and cats. All were communicating something and were surely heard and responded to by others of like kind or species.

Yet as far as I know only one species among them tried to befriend another. Anne's voice, in that sense, stood out from all the rest.

Perhaps that is one of the finest possibilities of human language—that we can speak in the hope of befriending all living things.

Patti's Compliment

Earlier this morning I saw Patti, who works in our retreat house. I had given her a batch of essays to read a while back, and she told me this morning how much she liked them. I was a bit embarrassed because I suppose I really do not think about my writing all that much. I thanked Patti and told her that her opinion meant a lot to me.

Later, I thought back on what Patti said. She is a warm and friendly person, and I admire her ease with people and how readily she shares her goodness in concrete ways. She accomplishes this every day by doing and saying and loving. I admire that.

And so I write about Patti, taking care with my words. For doing and saying and loving is what I most want to write about.

The Beautiful Flower

In a garden on the monastery grounds stands a large fountain. In front of the fountain once grew a large flower, the name of which I never knew. I would go to the garden very early in the morning, just before dawn, and at that early hour the petals of the flower were always closed. As I sat there, the sun would slowly rise and I would watch the flower carefully, hoping to see it open. It always stayed closed, however, and I soon would go back inside and forget about it.

If I returned several hours later, though, the flower would invariably be opened as fully as possible—so much so that its outer petals, almost the size of a sheet of paper, looked to be in danger of falling to the ground.

When I returned again later in the afternoon as the sun was setting, those same petals would have slowly risen to enclose the smaller petals and hide them once again for another night.

Erected right over the fountain is a sand casting of a lamb pierced with a sword. It is the ancient symbol of the Paschal Lamb, the Risen Christ—a simple and quite beautiful work of art. As I sat before the flower and the Lamb for so many hours, I imagined the flower to be humanlike, opening slowly to the presence and immediacy of the light and warmth of the sun and folding in upon itself as shelter from the cold and darkness.

It is God who gave life and beauty to that flower each day, and each night the Lamb silently graced the darkness of the garden as a reminder that life is present even when we might seek to hide from it.

Meghan's
Macaronis

There is a place deep in our woods at the monastery where I sit and read and write. It is just the right size to accommodate me and the few things that I bring with me.

I am never really alone in this place. My friends for that part of the day are the animals and insects that live there in abundance. Birds and frogs, ants and wandering cats, salamanders, snakes, squirrels and so many other "creeping things and winged fowl," as the psalm goes. The trees are tall, creating a canopy high above the forest floor that offers generous shade in the warmer months. And in the winter, with the branches bereft of their leaves, sunshine pours through. It is a place that truly speaks to my heart and soul in a language richer than human speech.

Indeed, the finest of human words, those of the poet, try to capture the language of nature in the medium of human letters, rhyme, syntax. Yet how to speak the wind, or phrase the sun, or turn the song of a bird into consonants and vowels? When I raise my head from my book or paper and feel all that is around me, I try to let it speak as only nature can.

A few days ago I was in my spot. It was early morning, and I was reading when I noticed a sound that I had not heard before. All around me was a soft crackling sound, not unlike the falling of snow on dry leaves in early winter. It was a clear morning, the sun was still rising, and the sound baffled me. As pervasive as it was, I could not determine what was causing it. Then I heard something hitting the pages of my book, and looking at the book that lay open on my knees I saw tiny flecks of brown. I picked one of them up and holding it close to my eyes saw that it was a seed. The trees around me—all of the same type of fir—were filled with cones that had opened and whose seeds were falling to the ground. It was a shower of new and promised life, the first beginnings of great things to become. The forest was replenishing itself.

I thought about how everything seemed so harmonious and connected that morning. Of course this kind of rebirth happens all the time, but I had never experienced it before as intently as that morning, when the seeds were literally falling on my head.

Saint Bernard of Clairvaux wrote long ago that "our works do not pass away; rather, they are scattered like temporal seeds of eternity. The fool will be astonished when he sees a great harvest shooting up from a little seed—good or bad harvest according to the different quality of the sowing. . . . So, practice random kindness and senseless acts of beauty."

I had Bernard's very words in my pocket the morning I heard the seeds falling. The words are printed on a card we give to guests who spend time in our retreat house.

I remember a meal I had with my sister Mary, her husband, Brian, and their family when I visited them in Switzerland one time. Mary had made cheese macaroni, and across from me sat my niece Meghan, who was then three years old. On a red plastic plate, which was at eye level with her on the table, Meghan had arranged her macaronis with great care, using her fingers to situate them just so. I can still see her face as she looked at me, giggled, and ate the macaronis one by one with a look of delight that is rare this side of Eden. Her pleasure was manifold: she loved the macaroni, loved her decorative style, loved me for coming to visit, loved eating without a fork, and obviously loved being three years old and having not a care in the world.

Not too long ago I reminded Meghan, now in her twenties, about that evening. Giggling in much the same way and taking a strand of blond hair from her eye in exactly the same gesture that she did back then, she said that she did not remember.

But I remember. I wonder how often Mary and Brian did little things for her like preparing that macaroni meal—a thousand, a hundred thousand, a million times? Like seeds dropped long ago, such little things have grown and now have a life of their own.

The Blue Radio

I once had the smallest of radios—actually it was what was called a crystal set—made of blue plastic. It was about half the size of a shoe box and had just two dials. I had ordered it from the back of a comic book, and it was one of the first things that I had ever purchased through the mail.

I must have been thirteen or fourteen years old at the time. The radio cost only a few dollars, which seemed like a lot of money to me back then. I so looked forward each day for the brown UPS truck.

One day, the small package arrived. The radio was wrapped, with special assembly directions for the all-important crystal. Putting it together was very easy. There were only a few pieces—the plastic body, an earphone and the crystal. To my delight, it really worked.

The crystal was capable of picking up only AM stations. It would be a few more years before FM became the more popular frequency for rock 'n' roll. Each night, I lay in bed with the small earpiece all but glued to my ear. I put it on my pillow and listened as I fell asleep. The copper wire sometimes came loose, but if I jiggled the wire just right, I was able to pick up such stations as WABC, WMCA and WINS, the three main rock stations at the time in the New York metropolitan area.

I remember one night in particular. A blizzard had struck the New York area, and it was a major one. As I lay in my bed that night, listening to music as the wind howled and the night sky was furious with snow, I became aware of the paradoxical stillness that a blizzard brings. Everything in the world had stopped, as far as I was concerned, except for the wind and the snow and the music.

I felt a sense of awe that through a wire and blue plastic I was connected to the world, in spite of the storm. It did not matter that the radio was small and inexpensive. For the comfort it brought me that night, I would not have traded it for the fanciest radio in the world.

Something so simple gave me incredible pleasure. As the years passed, my little crystal radio was replaced with large and more expensive sets that had rows of lights and dials. As much as I enjoyed later models, however, the innocence and pleasure of that first simple blue set contained a magic I never recaptured.

That was forty years—and so many songs—ago. I now live in a cloister, where there are no radios or televisions (and no snowstorms, either). Not long ago, while lying in bed one night waiting for sleep to come, I thought about that little blue radio and the simple but rich pleasures it brought me. Looking back, I think that it served a purpose that is becoming clearer to me as I pass my days and nights in monastic peace. In a sense, the little blue radio is still communicating something to me after all these years.

These days I must fine tune the receptor that is my heart. And on those nights that God seems far away, I need to jiggle the connection just a bit.

Grace Is Everywhere

I was recently home to visit my mother, who lives in Covington, Louisiana, in an assisted-care facility called Christwood. Mom has her own apartment, and the place is beautiful in many ways. She has friends in abundance, regular visits from my brothers and sisters, and her good health, except for an advanced case of macular degeneration that has left her legally blind.

I was there for two weeks, and since the apartment is small I slept on the couch in the living room. It was comfortable. Since coming to the monastery I have become used to a smaller bed on which to sleep.

I drove to Louisiana from Conyers, and the ride afforded me a chance to acclimate myself to returning to the hustle and bustle of American culture. It had been just over two years since I had last been home, and that was for Dad's funeral.

I was surprised, as the miles piled up on the odometer of the rented car, how accustomed I had become to the routine of monastic life and being pretty much in one place for most of the time. There is nothing particularly religious or sacred about that. What happens, though, is that the absence of most distractions makes room for the fullness of awareness. The monastic life—the smells of forest and incense, the sounds of bells, the rush of the wind, the cadence of the rain—seeps deeply into one's very pores. I experience these things with an attention that I never had before. It all adds up to a daily invitation that comes from all around me to be attentive, to listen, to see, to respond.

Monastic life grounds me. I know I am more at peace inside the monastery than outside. I also know that the monastery environment is not artificial. Human life is lived in the cloister: monks work, hope, suffer, celebrate and wonder like everyone else. What seems to me to be the biggest difference "in here"—as opposed to "out there"—is our commonly shared attempt to live as simple a life as possible.

Before I came to Conyers, I could easily plug my attention into a lot of things: television, the stereo, billions of words in countless conversations, running hither and yon with all sorts of things to do. That can happen in monastic life, too. A monk can lose himself in busyness. He can live from day to day or month to month and not take notice of all that is around him. But that has not been my experience.

Might I say that a Trappist monastery is a place where heart and memory become more expansive? They become free to roam terrains that are more natural to them. I have found in the nearly four years that I have been a monk that I have had to learn to pray in ways that I never did before. I have simply been given more of myself to deal with.

My memory now reaches far and wide. It seems as if it is looking for something, as if it has a life and intent all its own. It brings things back to me that I had long forgotten. A few days ago, I thought of a dog my family once had, Rusty, who would bound into the woods and come back with the oddest of things, a stick or a ball that had been thrown there weeks or years before. My memory seems to function like Rusty did. It goes off on its own and comes back with things I wasn't even looking for. The monastery has exposed my memory to a wide-open field—my past—and for the first time in my life it is free to run and retrieve what it fancies. I am trying to understand what to do with what it brings back, and writing helps.

As soon as I drove out of the car-rental place, I could immediately feel the pull of American culture around me. There were so many things demanding my attention—music on the radio, news broadcasts, advertisements, billboards. I was aware of the two-week limit of my stay, and I wanted to give Mom my undivided attention. I took her shopping, to the hairdresser, Clovis, to the drugstore, to visit relatives. We had quiet times, too—dinners and breakfasts and lunches when it was just the two of us. Yet even during those times, I yearned for a stillness that seemed to evade me. My mind and heart were always racing faster than I could understand. I did not say anything to Mom other than a comment or two on how quickly time goes.

One morning not very long into my stay, I awoke to the sound of a man's voice coming from the room where Mom has her television and her reading machine. I quietly got up and walked the few steps into the room, and there was Mom sitting as close as she could before the television set, watching a televised Mass that is broadcast daily from New Orleans. The celebrant that morning was the retired Archbishop of New Orleans, Phillip Hannon. It was his voice that I responded to; it is very distinctive and calm. Mom had her rosary beads in her hand. She could not see me, since I was behind her. I sat down quietly and prayed the rest of the Mass with her. Suddenly, I felt more at home than I could have ever imagined.

Praying quietly along with Mom, I felt connected to her, to those with whom she lives, to my sisters and brothers, to my Trappist brothers who were then far away. The language of the Mass helped me remember. It called me to something more than I could have found for myself that morning.

Not much later that same morning, still quite early, I went out on the little porch that Mom has at the front of her apartment and watched an elderly man walking his dog. I happened to meet him later, and he told me that he does that every morning. He calls that his "peaceful time." Whether or not he knew it, he expressed the contemplative need in all of us.

It may be tempting to say that a "religious" experience like the Mass is a more refined one than sitting on a porch or walking one's dog, but I think it is best to say that God finds us where we are. We were made to be with God and with each other in peace—walking our dogs, sipping a cup of coffee, praying before a TV set.

Today is early Sunday morning, Low Sunday according to the Psalter, the first Sunday after Easter. It is raining heavily. I wonder if Mom is just getting up from her chair after having watched the televised Mass. Is it raining in Covington, Louisiana? Is that man walking his little dog in the rain?

The dying priest in George Bernanos' *Diary of a Country Priest* sighed as he said, "Grace is everywhere."

Like the rain, we do not make grace fall into our lives. It just comes and comes again.

Afterword

The human being is a creature-in-search whose eternal compass is set to the interminable question "For what?" For what are we really searching in life? Where should we go to seek it? How will we know when we have found it?

The questions ring across time, through great literature, in popular music, behind every major work of art. Every culture, every spirituality, every wisdom figure in every arena of life concentrates on finding the answer to the secret of living, the endpoint of life. Whatever the magnet that draws them on, whatever the tradition that guides them, these seekers walk the same way, they beat a single path, and eventually they come to the same conclusion.

"The meaning of life is to see," as a Chinese proverb teaches. "Listen," the ancient Rule of Benedict instructs. "The real voyage of discovery consists not in seeking new landscapes," the philosopher Marcel Proust writes, "but in having new eyes."

It is not, in other words, so much where we go in life that matters, it is the way in which we immerse ourselves in it, open ourselves to it, see beyond its trappings wherever we are that measures the quality of the journey. This book by James Stephen Behrens is about that same kind of seeking, that same sort of seeing, that same depth of vision.

Grace Is Everywhere expands our vision. It proves the idea that where we are is sacred space, models the apocalypse of dailiness for us, gives us the opportunity to look again at the humdrum, the customary, the bland and the beautiful around us in order to find before our very eyes the edges of the eternal, the gleam of God in the obscure.

This book does two things: it focuses us on the present and it calls us to see beyond it, two elements of crucial importance in a world that is always on its way to somewhere else with nowhere else in mind. As a matter of fact, *Grace Is Everywhere,* written from the Trappist experience of the Rule of Benedict, the guiding spiritual tradition of Behrens' order, is a kind of survey of Benedictine spirituality.

Benedictine monasteries, you see, are not places where visions are expected. Benedictine monasteries are places where visions are considered unnecessary. What is not unnecessary in a Benedictine monastery, however—what is endemic to a Benedictine monastery, indeed— is the development of the contemplative heart, the heart that sees the world as God sees the world.

Monasteries, ironically, are places where

what is patently, palpably real—if the contemplation practiced there is real—is considered vision enough. This is a book about Benedictine/ Trappist monasticism that never mentions either the Rule of Benedict or monasticism at all. And that is as it should be. Monastics don't set out to be different from the rest of the world. They set out to be as finely focused of soul as a person can be and still walk the world. They set out to find God in the center of life. They set out to teach the neophyte in the spiritual life how to see what they search for in the very place they're searching for it. They set out to bring insight to what might otherwise be considered dense, in dearth of soul, too conventional to have anything to do with the glut of God.

Grace Is Everywhere presents us with the prototype of the monastic soul. Monasticism centers around six essential measures of human development: community, stewardship, prayer, silence, hospitality and stability. Behrens takes us into this network of monastic values and translates them for us. He shows us how they would look if we ever saw them alive and thriving in our own lives. And in the doing he enables us to look at our own lives again, this time with an eye for the transcendent in the midst of the pedestrian.

When a person begins to look at the world through monastic eyes, everything becomes the stuff of spirituality. Here, for instance, Behrens simply looks at the monastic enclosure in which he lives for models, samples, means of living the qualities that the Rule itself inspires. He talks about simple things, about common things, about the things we take for granted, and in the looking he unmasks for us the sacredness of the mundane. He rides through the monastery property and realizes that all of life is a process. He finds fullness in silence and teaches us that God speaks in the center of those who listen. He says goodby to his family in the monastery guest house and comes to understand that "relationships" are made out of more than blood ties. He talks to visitors and comes to understand that cloister is a quality of mind. He teaches us to see what we're looking at and think about what we're seeing. He leads us all to come to grips with the fact that sanctity is made from the stuff of the ordinary.

Grace Is Everywhere is a disarmingly simple work. At first glance, the book seems to lack a level of substance we've come to associate with erudite presentations of monastic spirituality. A little more thought, on the other hand, and the truth begins to dawn. It seeps into the cellars of the soul until suddenly it becomes clear that the real substance of monastic spirituality may lie in this very simplicity.

Learning to distinguish the real from the imaginary, bringing meaning to life, finding beauty where we have ceased to see may be the missing spiritual discipline of the age. It becomes so easy in an era of plastic relationships, shallow commitments, glittering consumption and human megalomania to substitute sacred rituals for serious reflection, churchgoing for morality, religion for spirituality. Then the meaning of monasticism becomes clear. Then the monastic mindset becomes new again, becomes the cornerstone of a society lost in complexities far beyond their merit. Then, a book like *Grace Is Everywhere* reminds us that life itself, real life, life lived in the commonplace, enriched by reflection and grounded in meaning, may be far simpler than we think.

Joan Chittister, OSB
Mount St. Benedict Monastery
Erie, Pennsylvania

Acknowledgments

I once asked my sister Mary where she thought vocations (of whatever kind) come from. Without a second's hesitation, she replied, "Everyone." Her words rang true, and I took them to heart.

So, where does a book come from? Everyone, obviously. All the people in my life have made this book possible.

But I would be remiss if I did not express special thanks to Michael Farrell and Tom Fox of the *National Catholic Reporter* who first published my writing and to Greg Pierce and everyone at ACTA Publications who have done so much to bring out my first book. And I must acknowledge Abbot Bernard Johnson, OCSO, and all my brother monks here at Conyers whom I am honored to know and love and with whom I now share my life.

Finally, I offer my deepest appreciation to Dolores Leckey and Sister Joan Chittester, OSB, who believed in me enough to contribute the Foreword and the Afterword to this book.

Good gifts come to everyone from everyone: vocations, books, life itself.

Additional Spirituality Resources

The Legend of the Bells and Other Tales
Stories of the Human Spirit
John Shea

Twenty-five of theologian and storyteller John Shea's favorite stories, with the author's reflections on what each
story is about and how it can be a window into the world
of spirit. (190-page paperback, $12.95)

An Epidemic of Joy
Stories in the Spirit of Jesus
Andrew M. Greeley and Mary Greeley Durkin
Foreword by John Shea

Seventy short stories from everyday life, each illuminating
a familiar gospel passage, that bring images of forgiveness, grace, hope, and joy to new generations of believ-
ers. (160-page paperback, $9.95)

Everyday People, Everyday Grace
Daily Meditations for Busy Christians
George R. Szews

Brief stories of ordinary people experiencing God's grace
in their everyday lives, coupled with a carefully chosen
scripture quotation for each day of the year. (368-page
paperback, $9.95)

A Contemporary Celtic Prayer Book
William John Fitzgerald
Foreword by Joyce Rupp

A prayer book that captures the distinctive flavor and sen-
sibility of traditional Celtic spirituality for today's Christians,
featuring both a simplified Liturgy of the Hours and a trea-
sury of Celtic blessings, prayers, and rituals for a variety of
occasions. (160-page hardcover, $16.95)

**Available from booksellers or call
800-397-2282 in the U.S. or Canada.**